**Please check all items for damages
before leaving the Library.
Thereafter you will be held
responsible for all injuries
to items beyond reasonable wear.**

INVASIVE SPECIES UNDERWATER

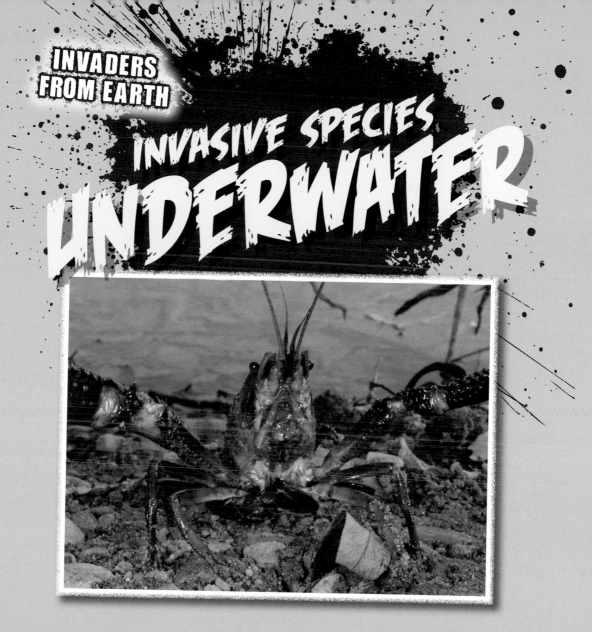

Richard Spilsbury

PowerKiDS press™
New York

Published in 2015 by **The Rosen Publishing Group**
29 East 21st Street, New York, NY 10010

Library of Congress Cataloging-in-Publication Data

Invasive species underwater / Richard Spilsbury.
        pages cm. – (Invaders from Earth)
  Includes bibliographical references and index.
ISBN 978-1-4994-0065-6 (pbk.)
ISBN 978-1-4994-0028-1 (6 pack)
ISBN 978-1-4994-0049-6 (library binding)
1. Introduced aquatic organisms–Juvenile literature. 2. Biological invasions–Juvenile
literature. 3. Environmental disasters–Juvenile literature. I. Title.
  QH90.8.I57S65 2015
  578.6'2–dc23

                                    2014027646

Produced for Rosen by Calcium
Editors for Calcium: Sarah Eason and Robyn Hardyman
Designer: Paul Myerscough

Photo credits: Cover: Shutterstock: Jose Gil; Inside: Dreamstime: Alessandrozocc 15b,
Lukas Blazek 10b, 11b, Richard Carey 7b, Anastas Dimitrov 16, Hans Peter Egert 23b,
Adrian Gilfillan 28t, Inavanhateren 17tr, Dennis Jacobsen 24b, Koulang 20, 20–21, Iuliia
Kryzhevska 18–19, Alexandr Malyshev 16–17, Micromann 12r, Oseland 8–9, Photawa 8,
Photoquest 9b, Ganna Poltoratska 18, Nick Saum 10–11, Ian Scott 28b, Toui2001 6b, WKSP
14, John Wollwerth 17tl, Michael Wood 26–27, 27t, 29, Y1413100419 14–15, Zaramira 24–25;
Shutterstock: Irina Afonskaya 21b, AJP 4–5, Steve Brigman 26, Rich Carey 2–3, 6–7, 30–31,
32, Miguel Azevedo e Castro 12, Fotogien 24l, Johnlips 11t, Dewald Kirsten 27b, Christian
Kohler 28–29, MG image and Design 13, Matteo Photos 1, 22b, 22–23, 23t, Samart
Mektippachai 21t, Jens Metschurat 12l, S-F 4b, Scubaluna 9t, Aleksey Stemmer 5b,
Vipavlenkoff 19, Richard Whitcombe 7t; Wikimedia Commons: James Gathany, CDC 15t,
Pavel Zuber 25t.

Manufactured in the United States of America

CPSIA Compliance Information: Batch CW15PK: For Further Information contact
Rosen Publishing, New York, New York at 1-800-237-9932

CONTENTS

WHAT ARE UNDERWATER INVADERS?

Rivers, lakes, and oceans around the world are under attack. They are being invaded by animals that arrive from faraway areas of water. These newcomers can cause serious problems for local wildlife and for people.

Unwanted Guests

Some underwater invaders are introduced on purpose by people who do not realize the damage they can do. They introduce these species for sport fishing or for food. They sometimes also release fish from their home aquariums into rivers or lakes, if they no longer want them.

AQUARIUM

Moved by Mistake

Some underwater invaders are introduced by accident. **Mollusks** grow on the bottoms of boats and are carried to new places when the boats move. Cargo ships carry water to help keep them stable when they are empty. This is called **ballast**. Sometimes animals are sucked into ballast water from the ocean. Other new species arrive in crates of fish that are transported to new places where they are sold.

Northern Pacific seastars were introduced into Australia by cargo ships from Japan. They eat **native** shellfish and cause problems for fisheries.

Around half of all the underwater alien species in the world travel to their new homes in ships.

5

LIONFISH

Lionfish are dangerous **predators**. They catch their **prey** by stretching out their fanlike fins to trap it. Then, they eat it.

On the Loose!

Lionfish originate from the South Pacific and Indian Oceans, but they are now found all along the East Coast of the United States. In the 1990s, a few lionfish were released by aquarium owners. Some escaped from pet stores damaged by Hurricane Andrew in 1992. Their numbers then grew quickly.

LIONFISH

Hungry as a Lion!

Lionfish are big eaters, and they are not fussy about what they eat. They eat more than 50 types of fish and other animals. Some are rare or valuable species, such as young spiny lobsters, wrasses, and parrotfish.

HUNGRY FISH

EARTH UNDER ATTACK

Lionfish can be dangerous to humans, too. The spines along a lionfish's back can sting you with a powerful **venom**. This causes pain, sweating, and breathing difficulties. The venom can even paralyze you, which means that you cannot move.

Lionfish are sometimes called zebrafish or firefish because of their stripes and colors.

7

ZEBRA MUSSEL

Zebra mussels are small mollusks that cause big problems. They arrived in the Great Lakes in the 1980s, in the ballast water of ships from Europe and Asia. Since then they have spread across North America.

Pipeline Problems

Zebra mussels cause trouble when they gather in large clusters. The clusters can block pipes that carry water, reducing the water flow. In just 1 square yard (0.8 sq m) of water there can be up to 700,000 zebra mussels clinging to boats and pipes.

Zebra mussels **reproduce** very quickly and have no natural predators in North America.

Killer Mussels

Zebra mussels also threaten the native species of mussels in an area, because they are more numerous. This is not good for local fish either, because zebra mussels are less **nutritious** than native mussels. When the fish eat only zebra mussels, they become undernourished and they decline, too.

ZEBRA MUSSEL

HOOVER DAM

EARTH UNDER ATTACK

Quagga mussels are a similar invader species to zebra mussels and cause similar problems. At the massive Hoover Dam in Nevada, electricity is generated. There, the quantity of quagga mussels has caused some electricity turbines to be temporarily shut down, cutting off the supply to 1.6 million electricity customers.

ASIAN CARP

Four types of carp are causing trouble in North America. They are bighead, black, grass, and silver carp. Together they are known as Asian carp.

On the Move

Asian carp are native to parts of eastern Asia. They were introduced to fish farms in North America in the 1960s and 1970s, to control weeds and other pests such as water snails. Floods carried them into the Mississippi River. Since then, they have spread to other waterways in the United States.

Asian carp can jump over barriers such as low dams to spread to new places.

Carp Conflicts

Asian carp eat large amounts of plankton, which native fish also need to eat. In places where there are too many Asian carp, the quality of the water is reduced. This can kill off sensitive species such as freshwater mussels. Asian carp have also injured people in boats, because the noise of the propellers makes the carp jump high out of the water.

PLANKTON

BIGHEAD CARP

INVADER ANALYSIS

Asian carp can **be more than 3 feet (1 m) long.** They can eat **up to 40 times their body weight in plankton each day.**

GREEN CRAB

Some people call the European green crab the "cockroach of the sea" because, like the cockroach, it seems to be almost impossible to kill.

GREEN CRAB CLAW

GREEN CRAB

Armored Alien

This tough creature can live out of water for up to 1 week, even when it is hot. It can survive in freshwater for short periods of time. It can also survive in temperatures below zero and above 86°F (30°C). If the crab gets cold, it burrows into the sand for warmth.

Green and Greedy

The green crab eats almost anything: oysters, mussels, marine worms, and small crustaceans. It is fast and aggressive, and crushes shellfish in its huge front claws. It eats so much that it can damage clam and crab fisheries. It also robs native species of foods that they need.

EARTH UNDER ATTACK

The green crab is native to Europe and northern Africa. It has spread by ballast water and by being sold as bait or food. It is now found in North America, Australia, parts of South America, and South Africa.

In some places, the aggressive green crab is also known as the angry crab.

MOSQUITO FISH

The mosquito fish is native to the southern United States, but it was introduced across the world partly to feed on young mosquitoes in water. Adult mosquitoes can cause harm by spreading a disease called malaria. However, the mosquito fish turned out to be no better at controlling mosquitoes than native fish. Instead, it became a dangerous pest itself.

Mosquito fish are aggressive and often attack other fish.

Vicious Attacks

The mosquito fish attacks and sometimes kills other fish by nipping at and shredding their fins. It also harms small local fish by eating their young and by competing with them for food.

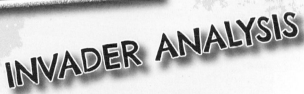
YOUNG MOSQUITO

Fewer Frogs

Mosquito fish also harm frogs, including rare species such as the **endangered** yellow-spotted tree frog of Australia. They eat the frogs' eggs and tadpoles.

INVADER ANALYSIS

Mosquito fish reproduce quickly. Females can have up to 300 young at one time. They have up to nine broods each year. Young mosquito fish become adults in less than 2 months.

MOSQUITO FISH

SEA WALNUT

Sea walnuts are tiny, see-through comb jellies. They are sometimes called sea gooseberries because of the hairs along their bodies. The hairs help the sea walnuts swim.

BLACK SEA

Fish Losses

The number of fish in the Black Sea, on the coast of Turkey, had already been reduced by **pollution** and **overfishing** before sea walnuts invaded. When the sea walnuts arrived, they began to eat the fish eggs, larvae, and other animals that fish rely on for food. The number of fish in the Black Sea then fell by 90 percent.

SEA WALNUT

Sea walnuts look a little like gooseberries! They may look cute, but these creatures are ferocious eaters.

Fighting Back

Sea walnuts increased in numbers because they had so much to eat. To get rid of them and increase the numbers of fish again, people introduced a different kind of comb jelly that eats sea walnuts!

EARTH UNDER ATTACK

The sea walnut is native to the Atlantic coast of North and South America. It was introduced to the Black Sea in the 1980s, in ballast water in empty oil tankers from the United States. Since then, it has spread into the Mediterranean Sea, the Marmara Sea, the Aegean Sea, and the Caspian Sea.

17

VEINED RAPA WHELK

The veined rapa whelk is a beautiful but deadly sea snail. It destroys other shellfish wherever it invades.

Rapa Routes

Veined rapa whelks are native to the northwest Pacific Ocean. They have spread worldwide in ballast water carried by ships. They first appeared in the Black Sea, then in Chesapeake Bay in the United States and the River Plate estuary in Argentina. The veined rapa whelk is now also found throughout Europe.

The veined rapa whelk has a very distinctive orange opening on its shell. The thick shell can grow as large as a grapefruit.

Whelk Warfare

Rapa whelks eat mussels, oysters, and clams in two different ways. Small whelks drill into the shells to reach the flesh inside. Larger whelks pry the shells open. The whelks are eaten by octopuses. However, octopuses are absent in the places that the whelks have invaded, which is why they have increased so greatly in number.

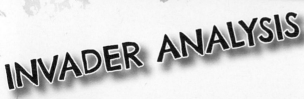
WHELKS

INVADER ANALYSIS

Veined rapa whelks have some benefits. People can eat them instead of the shellfish the whelks have killed off. Hermit crabs are increasing in some places because they can live inside the empty shells of veined rapa whelks.

SNAKEHEAD FISH

The northern snakehead is often called the Frankenfish because of its ferocious habits. This monster has long, sharp teeth, and eats fish, birds, and other small animals.

Frankenfish

The northern snakehead fish is native to parts of Russia, China, and Korea. It probably spread by being bought live from fish markets or pet stores and later released into lakes or rivers. It is now found in several US states, including Virginia, Maryland, Pennsylvania, and New York.

Snakeheads are a favorite food in many parts of Asia.

FISH FEAST

Unstoppable?

The snakehead is an almost indestructible fish that threatens and kills other water wildlife. The fish can survive in freezing temperatures and can live out of the water for up to 4 days. The snakehead has even been seen traveling over short distances by wiggling its body.

SNAKEHEAD FISH

INVADER ANALYSIS

The snakehead fish has a torpedo-shaped body and a small head covered in large scales, which make it look like a snake. It grows up to 5 feet (1.5 m) long and weighs up to 15 pounds (7 kg).

RED SWAMP CRAYFISH

The red swamp crayfish is native to the south-central United States. It was introduced to Europe for food and quickly spread there. It is a problem because it is wiping out local species of crayfish.

Crayfish Killers

The red swamp crayfish is larger and more aggressive than native European species of crayfish. It can be easily identified by its huge front claws, which are red underneath. It kills local crayfish by taking most of their food. It also carries a **fungus** that spreads a disease that kills other crayfish.

EUROPEAN CRAYFISH

INVADER ANALYSIS

In the United Kingdom, the red swamp crayfish has **wiped** out almost 95 percent of native, **white-clawed** crayfish species since it was introduced in the late 1970s.

RED SWAMP CRAYFISH

Doing Damage

Red swamp crayfish affect other local wildlife by eating fish eggs and small underwater **invertebrates**. They also damage the muddy banks of ponds, ditches, canals, and rivers by digging deep burrows with their large front claws. They burrow to find food and shelter.

Mallards and some other birds eat red swamp crayfish, but they cannot control their populations.

NILE PERCH

The Nile perch is one of the largest freshwater fish in the world. The fish has razor-sharp teeth and is a fierce predator that kills almost any animal that it sees.

Cichlid Killers

The Nile perch is native to Ethiopia in Africa. It was introduced to other African lakes and rivers, such as Lake Victoria in East Africa, for sport fishing. In Lake Victoria it caused the **extinction** of many types of rare cichlid fish and other local species.

NILE PERCH

CICHLID FISH

Greedy Giant

This greedy giant eats a variety of prey including crustaceans, mollusks, insects, and fish. This means it can destroy the populations of many native animals in a lake or river. In Queensland, Australia, people can be heavily fined for keeping a living Nile perch, because it threatens the native Barramundi fish.

The Nile perch can swallow many different animals in its large mouth.

INVADER ANALYSIS

The Nile perch can **live** for **up** to 16 years. It can grow to **more than** 6 **feet (2 m) long** and **weigh up to** 500 pounds (225 kg).

LARGEMOUTH BASS

Largemouth bass are big fish that anglers love to catch, so people have introduced them into rivers worldwide. The problem is that largemouth bass will eat any animals that they find in the water.

A largemouth bass's lower jaw is so long it can stretch beyond the fish's eye. The jaw hinges forward and upward when the bass opens its mouth.

Big Mouth

Largemouth bass feed day and night. They eat insects and fish, such as salmon and trout, as well as birds that fall into the water. Their mouths stretch wide to swallow their food whole. Their speed, size, and sharp spines protect the fish from predators.

Good Parents

Largemouth bass have successfully invaded new places because they care for their young. They guard their nests to stop other fish eating their eggs. Because of this, numerous young largemouth bass hatch and grow into adults.

LARGEMOUTH BASS

EARTH UNDER ATTACK

Largemouth bass are native to areas of the United States east of the Rocky Mountains. They were introduced to other parts of the United States and to other countries, such as Japan and South Africa, from the nineteenth century onward. Since then, they have spread far and wide. Today they are one of the most widely distributed fish in the world.

NEW INVASIONS

We need our oceans, lakes, and rivers to stay healthy, but **invasive species** are destroying native plants and animals. They are also costing millions of dollars to control. How can we stop new invasions?

Stopping Invaders

It is difficult to get rid of new species once they are established, so the best way to solve the problem is to stop species spreading to new areas in the first place. By 2016, all ships will have to clean their ballast water of unwanted living things. They can do this with chemicals or by heating the water.

EMPTYING BALLAST WATER

Checking Ships

At ports where ships come and go, ship hulls and containers should be inspected closely. Any cargo that might contain stowaway animals should also be inspected. Another solution is to impose tough fines on people who illegally buy and sell exotic fish and other water wildlife.

Asian carp include nine different species. Grass carp (right) is one of these species.

INVADER ANALYSIS

Experts think that it will take many years and cost billions of dollars to stop the Asian carp that are invading the Great Lakes. They are threatening the area's important fishing industry.

GLOSSARY

ballast Water or another heavy substance in a ship's hull that helps keep it stable in the water.

endangered In danger of dying out completely.

extinction The dying out of a plant or animal.

fungus A type of living thing that includes yeasts, mushrooms, toadstools, and molds.

invasive species A kind of plant or animal not native to an area and causing it harm.

invertebrates Animals without backbones.

mollusks Types of animals that include slugs, snails, squids, and octopuses.

native Born in or belonging to a particular place.

nutritious Containing many substances the body needs for good health.

overfishing Catching too many fish.

pollution Substances that make water, land, or air dirty and unsafe to use.

predators Animals that hunt and eat other animals.

prey An animal that is hunted and eaten by other animals.

reproduce To produce babies.

venom A poison produced by an animal.

FURTHER READING

Books

Drake, Jane. *Alien Invaders: Species That Threaten Our World.* Toronto, ON, Canada: Tundra Books, 2008.

Latta, Sarah L. *Keep Out! Invasive Species* (Nature's Invaders). North Mankato, MN: Capstone Press, 2014.

Monroe Peterson, Judy. *Marine Biologists* (Underwater Explorers). New York, NY: Rosen Publishing Group, 2009.

Websites

Due to the changing nature of Internet links, PowerKids Press has developed an online list of websites related to the subject of this book. This site is updated regularly. Please use this link to access the list:
www.powerkidslinks.com/ife/water

INDEX